My First Dictionary

Written by
Betty Root

Illustrated by
**Mark Ruffle, Jenny Snape,
and Jonathan Langley**

DK

A Dorling Kindersley Book

DK | Penguin Random House

DK UK
Senior Editor Dawn Sirett
Project Art Editor Victoria Palastanga
Category Publisher Sue Leonard
Jacket Designers Victoria Harvey, Ian Midson
Design Development Manager Helen Senior
Publishing Director Mary-Clare Jerram
Production Editor Marc Staples
Production Controller Jen Lockwood

DK India
Editors Manasvi Vohra, Janashree Singha,
Nidhilekha Mathur
Art Editor Nitu Singh
Assistant Art Editors Vikas Sachdeva,
Rohit Walia
DTP Designers Anurag Trivedi,
Arjinder Singh, Arvind Kumar
Picture Researcher Sakshi Saluja
Managing Editor Glenda Fernandes
Managing Art Editor Navidita Thapa
CTS Manager Sunil Sharma

First published in Great Britain in 1993 as
DK First Dictionary
This edition published in Great Britain in 2016, as part of
Everything You Need to Know: Key Stage 1
By Dorling Kindersley Limited
80 Strand, London WC2R 0RL

Copyright © 1993, © 2012, © 2016
Dorling Kindersley Limited
A Penguin Random House Company

13 14 15 16 17 10 9 8 7 6 5 4 3 2 1
001 – 297998 – May/2016

A CIP catalogue record for this book is
available from the British Library

ISBN: 978-0-2412-8038-6

Printed in China

A WORLD OF IDEAS:
SEE ALL THERE IS TO KNOW

Contents

Notes for parents and teachers

My First Dictionary is a colourful introduction to the world of words and their meanings for young children. Packed with photographs and bright illustrations, this book is designed to encourage children to practise using a dictionary, and to learn more about the language they use every day.

About this book

Each of the 1,000 headwords featured in **My First Dictionary** has been carefully selected from words commonly used by young children. Every headword is clearly defined in simple language and further defined with a colour photograph or illustration. When teaching young children language and dictionary usage, it is essential to provide them with accurate visual clues to help them identify the word they want. With this in mind, every image in **My First Dictionary** has been carefully chosen to help young children understand each word.

Learning the alphabet

In the beginning, this dictionary will be a book to share with your child. Young children need to learn the letters of the alphabet and to understand alphabetical order, and this picture dictionary is an ideal tool for discovering how the alphabet works. While you are looking at the pictures with your child, point to the highlighted letter (picked out on white) in the alphabet strip at the top of each page. Then point to each headword as you name the pictures. In this way, children will learn that there are groups of words that begin with the same letter, and sometimes the same sound.

Learning to read and spell

As children develop into more competent readers, they will enjoy using **My First Dictionary** independently. Children will be able to find out for themselves what a particular word means, or how to spell it. However, this goal is best achieved with the support of parents and teachers.

Learning to use a dictionary

There is an exciting selection of word games at the back of this book. These games have been specially devised to help children understand the purpose of a dictionary and to become confident users. By working through these language games together, you will encourage your child to learn dictionary skills through play.

To broaden children's vocabulary, there are more than 150 additional words that appear in **bold** type in some of the definitions, or that can be found in some of the picture labels. These words are listed in an index on page 96. This index provides young readers with the possibility of gaining cross-referencing skills, which will help them to work confidently with other dictionaries.

By looking at the pages of **My First Dictionary** with young children, you will provide them with a head start in reading and writing, and an enjoyable look at language.

Betty Root, Author

A a

above

When something is **above** something else, it is higher up. These birds are flying above the trees.

accident

An **accident** is something that happens by mistake.

acrobat

An **acrobat** is a person who can do gymnastics and clever balancing tricks. Some acrobats can balance on their heads or walk on their hands.

act

To **act** is to pretend to be someone else. An **actor** is a person who acts in a play in front of an audience. Some actors act in television programmes and films.

add

To **add** is to find the sum total of two or more numbers.

address

Janet Brown
14 Elm Road
New Town

An **address** describes where a person lives or works. It can include the number or name of a building, a street name, and the name of a town or a village.

adult

An **adult** is a grown-up person. **Men** and **women** are adults. When you are older, you will become an adult.

aeroplane

An **aeroplane** is a flying machine with wings. It flies people and packages quickly from one place to another.

airport

An **airport** is a place where aeroplanes take off and land.

alligator

An **alligator** is a reptile with thick, scaly skin, lots of sharp **teeth**, and a broad head.

alphabet

abcdefg

English alphabet

абвгдеж

Russian alphabet

An **alphabet** is a list of all the letters we use to write words. Different languages have different alphabets.

ambulance

An **ambulance** is a special vehicle that is used to carry sick or injured people to a hospital.

anchor

An **anchor** is a large, metal hook on a long chain. It digs into the bottom of the sea to hold a ship in place.

angry

An **angry** person is someone who feels very cross about something.

animal

An **animal** is any living thing that is not a plant. You are an animal, and so is a fish, a spider, a bird, a snake, and a dog.

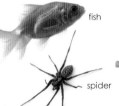

fish

spider

bird

snake

girl

dog

ant

An **ant** is a tiny insect. Ants live in nests under the ground.

ape

An **ape** is an animal that is similar to a monkey, but without a tail.

apple

An **apple** is a fruit that grows on an apple tree.

aquarium

An **aquarium** is a tank of water in which fish, other water creatures, and plants are kept.

arm

Your **arm** is the part of your body between your shoulder and your hand.

armadillo

An **armadillo** is an animal covered with hard, bony scales. These scales protect the armadillo from attack.

armour

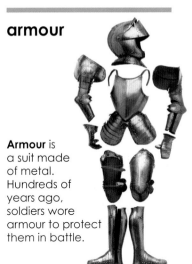

Armour is a suit made of metal. Hundreds of years ago, soldiers wore armour to protect them in battle.

army

An **army** is a large group of soldiers who are trained to fight on land in times of war.

arrow

An **arrow** is a sign that points the way.

artist

An **artist** is a person who creates art. Some artists draw or paint pictures. Other artists make pots out of clay, or statues out of stone.

astronaut

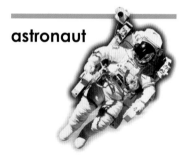

An **astronaut** is a person who travels to outer space in a spacecraft. Some astronauts have walked on the surface of the moon.

athlete

An **athlete** is a person who is good at sports, such as running, jumping, or swimming. Athletes take part in races or competitions.

audience

An **audience** is a group of people watching a performance together.

author

An **author** is a person who writes stories or other texts.

avalanche

An **avalanche** is a sudden fall of snow and rocks down the side of a mountain.

baby

A **baby** is a very young child.

back

The **back** of something is the part behind the front.

back

Your **back** is the part of your body that is behind your chest. Your back is between your neck and your bottom.

bake

To **bake** something is to cook it in an oven. A **baker** is a person who makes bread and cakes in a **bakery**.

ball

A **ball** is used to play some games and sports. Most balls are round.

balloon

A **balloon** is a thin rubber bag that is blown up with air or another kind of gas.

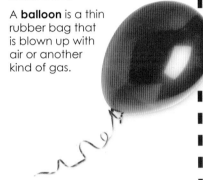

banana

A **banana** is a long, curved fruit with a yellow skin. Bananas grow in bunches on banana plants.

band

A **band** is a group of people playing musical instruments together.

bandage

A **bandage** is a strip of material that is used to cover an injury.

bank

A **bank** is the high ground on both sides of a river or a stream.

bank

A **bank** is a safe place where you can keep money. You can take your money out again when you need it.

barbecue

A **barbecue** is a meal you cook outside on an open fire.

barn

A **barn** is a large farm building where a farmer keeps machinery or animals.

baseball

Baseball is a game played with a bat and a ball by two teams of nine players.

basket

A **basket** is a container made of woven strips of material.

bat

A **bat** is a kind of stick or racket that is used to hit a ball.

bat

A **bat** is a small, furry animal with wings. Bats sleep during the day hanging upside down. They hunt for food at night.

bath

A **bath** is a container that you fill with water and sit in to wash yourself. A **bathroom** is the room where you take a bath.

battery

A **battery** is a sealed case that makes electricity.

beach

A **beach** is a strip of land by the edge of a sea or a lake. Beaches are covered with sand or pebbles.

beak

A **beak** is the hard, pointed part of a bird's mouth.

bear

A **bear** is a large, heavy animal with thick fur and strong claws.

beard

A **beard** is the hair that grows on a man's chin and cheeks.

bed

A **bed** is a piece of furniture that you sleep on. A **bedroom** is the room where you go to sleep.

bee

A **bee** is a flying insect. Some bees collect nectar, the sweet liquid in flowers, and turn it into honey.

beetle

A **beetle** is an insect. Beetles have hard, shiny wing cases to protect the soft parts of their bodies. Most beetles can fly.

behind

When something is **behind** something else, it is at the back of it. This girl is standing behind the door.

bell

A **bell** is a hollow, cup-shaped piece of metal. When you shake it, the striker inside makes the bell ring.

below

When something is **below** something else, it is lower down. This bulb is growing below the surface of the **soil**.

surface of soil

bulb

belt

A **belt** is a strap that you wear around your **waist**.

bench

A **bench** is a **seat** for more than one person.

berry

A **berry** is a soft, juicy, stoneless fruit.

between

When you are **between** two things, you are in the middle of them. This boy is lying between the two dogs.

bicycle

A **bicycle** is a machine with two wheels that are moved around by **pedals**. To ride a **bike** you sit on the **seat**, pedal with your **feet**, and steer using the **handlebars**.

handlebars

seat

training wheels

pedal

wheel

big

When something is **big**, it is not small. The yellow spotty ball is bigger than the blue spotty ball.

binoculars

Binoculars are a special kind of glasses. They make things that are far away look bigger and closer.

bird

A **bird** is an animal with feathers, two wings, and a beak. Most birds can fly.

birthday

Your **birthday** is the day of the year when you were born. You may be given birthday cards and eat birthday cake on this special day.

bite

To **bite** something is to take hold of it with your **teeth**.

black

Black is a very dark colour. It is the opposite of white.

blanket

A **blanket** is a thick cover that keeps you warm in bed.

blind

A person who is **blind** cannot see. **Guide dogs** help blind people to walk about safely.

blood

Blood is the red liquid that is pumped around your body by your heart.

blossom

Blossom is the flower that grows on a plant, especially a fruit tree.

apple blossom

blouse

A **blouse** is clothing worn by a girl or a woman on the top part of her body.

blow

To **blow** is to push air quickly out of your mouth. This boy is blowing bubbles.

blue

Blue is the colour of the sky on a sunny day.

boat

A **boat** is a small ship. Boats carry people and things across water.

body

head

shoulder

hand

chest

arm

leg

foot

Your **body** is every part of you.

bone

A **bone** is one of the pieces of a skeleton. You have 206 different bones in your body.

book

A **book** is a collection of pages held together between two covers. Words and pictures can be printed on the pages of a book.

boomerang

A **boomerang** is a flat, curved piece of wood. When you throw a boomerang, it turns around in the air and comes back to you.

bottle

A **bottle** is a glass or plastic container for drinks and other liquids.

bottom

The **bottom** of something is the lowest part of it.

bowl

A **bowl** is a deep, round dish to put food in.

box

A **box** is a container with straight sides, a bottom, and sometimes a top.

boy

A **boy** is a **male** child.

brain

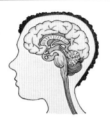

Your **brain** is inside your head. You think with your brain and it controls your body.

branch

A **branch** is a part of a tree that grows from the tree's **trunk**.

branch

trunk

bread

Bread is a food that is made from a mixture of water, flour or meal, and sometimes yeast.

break

When something **breaks**, it often cracks into pieces.

breakfast

Breakfast is the first meal that you eat in the day.

brick

A **brick** is a block of baked, hard clay used for building.

bride

A **bride** is a woman who is getting married. The man she is marrying is the **bridegroom.** After the wedding, they are **wife** and **husband.**

bridge

A **bridge** is built over a river, a railway, or a road so that people or traffic can get across.

bulldozer

A **bulldozer** is a powerful machine that is used to move heavy rocks and **soil.**

brown

Brown is a colour. Wood and **soil** are often brown.

brush

A **brush** is a tool that has a lot of bristles. A **hairbrush** is used to brush your hair. Other kinds of brushes are used for sweeping, painting, or cleaning.

building

A **building** is a place with walls and a roof, where people live or work. **Builders** use bricks, concrete, stones, or wood to **build** buildings.

burglar

A **burglar** is a person who breaks into a building to steal something.

burn

To **burn** something is to set it on fire.

bucket

A **bucket** is a container with a handle that is used to hold water or other things.

bulb

A **bulb** is a part of some plants. It grows underground.

bulb

A light **bulb** uses electricity to create light.

bus

A **bus** is a large vehicle that carries a lot of people. The bus **driver** stops at a **bus stop** to let the passengers get on and off.

bud

A **bud** is a young leaf or flower before it opens.

butcher

A **butcher** is a person who cuts up meat and sells it.

butter

Butter is a yellow, fatty food that is made from cream.

butterfly

A **butterfly** is a flying insect with four colourful wings.

button

A **button** is a small object used for fastening clothes.

buy

To **buy** is to give money for something so that it belongs to you. The boy is buying groceries.

Cc

cabbage

A **cabbage** is a vegetable with tightly packed leaves.

cabin

A **cabin** is a wooden house, often made from logs.

cactus

A **cactus** is a prickly plant that grows in the desert. Most cacti store water in their thick stems.

calculator

A **calculator** is a machine that you use to work with numbers.

calendar

A **calendar** is a chart that shows what day it is. Calendars also show the month and the year.

camel

A **camel** is a large animal with one or two humps on its back. Camels live in hot, dry deserts.

camera

A **camera** is a machine used for taking photographs.

camp

To **camp** is to live outside. A **campsite** is a place where you set up your camping equipment.

carrot

A **carrot** is a long vegetable that grows underground.

can

A **can** is a sealed, metal container for storing food.

car

A **car** is a vehicle with four wheels and an engine. People travel in cars from one place to another. A **car park** is a place where a lot of cars can park.

carry

To **carry** something is to take it from one place to another.

candle

A **candle** is a stick of wax with a string through the middle. When you burn a candle, it gives off a bright light.

carnation

A **carnation** is a flower with lots of petals. It can be various colours.

canoe

A **canoe** is a long, narrow boat that is moved through water with a paddle.

carpenter

A **carpenter** is a person who builds things out of wood. Some carpenters help to build houses. Other carpenters make furniture.

castle

A **castle** is a large building with thick, stone walls and tall towers. Castles were built hundreds of years ago to keep people safe from their enemies. Kings and queens lived in castles.

cap

A **cap** is a soft hat. This is a baseball cap.

cat

A **cat** is a furry animal that is often kept as a pet.

catch

To **catch** is to grab hold of something as it comes towards you.

caterpillar

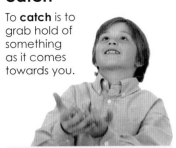

A **caterpillar** is a hairy insect that turns into a butterfly or a moth.

cauliflower

A **cauliflower** is a vegetable with green leaves and a white centre.

cave

A **cave** is a large hole in the side of a rock or under the ground.

centipede

A **centipede** is a tiny animal with many pairs of legs.

cereal

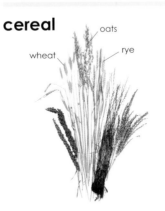

oats

wheat

rye

Cereal is a kind of grass that is grown for its grain. The grain is used to make food, such as flour or breakfast cereal.

chair

A **chair** is a piece of furniture for one person to sit on.

chameleon

A **chameleon** is a type of lizard that can change its skin colour to blend in with its surroundings. This chameleon has turned green to match the leaves.

champion

A **champion** is a person who wins a game, a competition, or a sporting event.

chase

To **chase** is to run after someone or something. These children are chasing the ball.

cheap

£20.00

£1.00

When something is **cheap**, you can buy it with a small amount of money.

15

checkout

A **checkout** is a counter in a supermarket where you go to pay for what you want.

cheer

To **cheer** is to shout and wave your hands with excitement.

cheese

Cheese is a food made from milk.

cheetah

A **cheetah** is a large, wild cat with a spotty coat. A cheetah can run faster than any other animal in the world.

chess

Chess is a game played on a chessboard.

chest

Your **chest** is the front part of your body, between your neck and your stomach.

chicken

cockerel

hen

chicks

A **chicken** is a type of farm bird. A female chicken is called a **hen**, a male chicken is called a **cockerel**, and a baby chicken is called a **chick**.

child

A **child** is a young boy or girl. **Children** grow up to become adults.

chimney

A **chimney** is a long pipe on top of a building. It takes away the smoke from a fire.

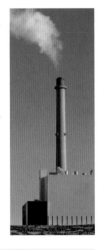

chimpanzee

A **chimpanzee** is a kind of ape. Chimpanzees live in groups and play games together like humans do.

chin

Your **chin** is the part of your face below your mouth.

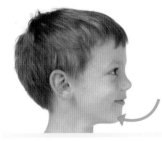

chocolate

Chocolate is a sweet food made from cocoa and sugar.

choir

A **choir** is a large group of people who sing together.

choose

To **choose** is to pick one thing instead of another.

chopstick

Chopsticks are two thin sticks that you use to pick up and eat food.

church

A **church** is a building where Christian people meet to pray and to sing hymns.

circle

A **circle** is a shape. Circles are round.

city

A **city** is a large town with lots of buildings where people live and work.

clap

To **clap** is to bring your hands together and make a loud noise.

claw

A **claw** is the sharp, hooked nail on the foot of a bird or an animal.

clean

When something is **clean**, it is not dirty. One boot is clean, but the other is muddy.

cliff

A **cliff** is a high, steep rock face.

climb

To **climb** is to go to the top of something using your hands and feet.

clock

A **clock** is a machine that shows you the time.

clothes

skirt

trousers   dress   shirt

Clothes are the things that people wear. Clothes are usually made from **cloth**.

cloud

A **cloud** is made out of drops of water floating in the sky.

clown

A **clown** is a funny person who makes people laugh. Clowns wear colourful clothes and paint their faces.

coat

A **coat** is an item of clothing that you wear outdoors to keep yourself warm.

cobweb

A **cobweb** is a net made by a spider to catch flies.

cockpit

A **cockpit** is the part of an aeroplane where the pilot sits. All the controls for flying the aeroplane are in the cockpit.

coconut

A **coconut** is a hard-shelled fruit with white flesh and coconut milk inside. Coconuts grow on coconut palm trees.

coffee

Coffee is a drink made from the roasted, crushed seeds of the coffee bush. Many people drink hot coffee in the morning or at the end of a meal.

coffee seeds (known as coffee beans)

cold

When something is **cold**, it is not hot. When the weather is cold you may feel chilly and wear a coat.

colour

Red, blue, and yellow are **colours**, and there are many other colours, bright, dark, and light.

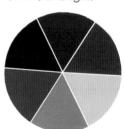

compact disc

A **compact disc**, or **CD**, is a circle of aluminium-coated plastic that stores a lot of sounds and pictures. A **compact disc player** is a machine used for playing some CDs.

computer

screen
mouse
keyboard

A **computer** is a machine that people use for writing, working with numbers, and storing information. You use a **keyboard** to bring up the information on the **screen.**

conductor

A **conductor** is a person who keeps an orchestra playing together.

cone

A **cone** is a solid shape that is round at one end and pointed at the other.

continent

A **continent** is a large piece of land. We divide the world into seven continents:
1 Africa
2 Antarctica
3 Asia
4 Australia
5 Europe
6 North America
7 South America

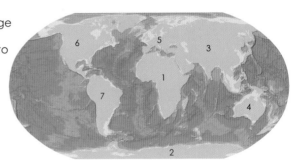

cook

To **cook** is to heat food and make it ready to eat.

corner

A **corner** is the point where two lines meet. This shape has three corners.

cotton

Cotton is the white fibre that grows on a cotton plant. Cotton is woven into **cloth.**

count

To **count** is to say numbers one after the other.

1   2   3

country

A **country** is a large area of land that is surrounded by borders and has its own special laws. **France** is a country.

France

cousin

uncle
aunt
cousins

A **cousin** is a child of your aunt or uncle. An **aunt** is a sister of your mother or father. An **uncle** is a brother of your mother or father.

cow

cow

calf

A **cow** is a large farm animal that gives us milk to drink. Cows are female **cattle**. Male cattle are called **bulls** and young cattle are called **calves.**

crab

A **crab** is a sea animal with large claws on its front legs. Crabs have a hard shell to protect their soft bodies.

crane

A **crane** is a tall machine with a long arm that is used to lift heavy things.

crawl

To **crawl** is to move around on your hands and knees.

crayon

A **crayon** is a stick of coloured wax that you use for drawing.

cricket

Cricket is a team game that is played with a cricket bat and ball.

cricket

A **cricket** is a small insect that chirps by rubbing its wings together.

crocodile

A **crocodile** is an animal with large jaws, a narrow head, and a powerful tail that helps it to swim.

crow

A **crow** is a bird with black feathers and a strong, black beak.

crowd

A **crowd** is a large number of people together in one place.

crown

A **crown** is a round headdress, often made of gold and jewels, worn by kings and queens.

crutch

A **crutch** is a long metal or wooden stick that helps you to walk.

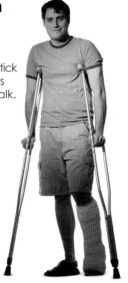

cry

When you **cry**, tears run down your face. Crying shows that you are sad or hurt.

cube

A **cube** is a solid shape with six square sides.

cucumber

A **cucumber** is a long, thin vegetable with a bumpy, green skin.

cup

A **cup** is a container that you drink from.

cupboard

A **cupboard** is a piece of furniture with doors on the front. You store things in a cupboard.

curtain

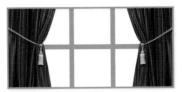

A **curtain** is a piece of material that hangs over or around a window. Curtains can be pulled across to cover a window.

cushion

A **cushion** is a cloth bag full of soft material or feathers. We sit or rest on cushions.

cut

To **cut** something is to slice it into pieces.

Dd

daffodil

A **daffodil** is a yellow spring flower that grows from a bulb.

daisy

A **daisy** is a flower with white petals and a yellow centre.

dam

A **dam** is a strong wall built across a river. A dam holds back water to make a lake.

dance

To **dance** is to move your body in time to music.

deer

A **deer** is a large, shy animal that can run very fast. A female deer is called a **doe** and a young deer is called a **fawn**. Male deer are called **stags** and have **antlers**.

antlers

stags

dandelion

A **dandelion** is a yellow wild flower.

dentist

A **dentist** is a person who takes care of your teeth.

dessert

A **dessert** is any kind of sweet food that you eat at the end of a meal.

day

A **day** is 24 **hours** long. **Morning, afternoon, evening,** and night are all parts of one day.

morning   afternoon

evening   night

desert

A **desert** is a hot, dry, sandy area of land.

detective

A **detective** is someone who hunts for clues and solves crimes.

deaf

To be **deaf** is to have difficulty hearing. Some deaf people use sign language to talk to each other.

desk

A **desk** is a type of table that you sit at to read and write.

diagram

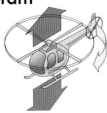

A **diagram** is a detailed drawing that explains how something works.

diamond

A **diamond** is a valuable stone that sparkles. It is clear like glass.

diary

A **diary** is a small notebook in which you write what has happened during your day.

dictionary

A **dictionary** is a book with a list of words and their meanings arranged in alphabetical order. This book is a dictionary.

different

When two things are **different**, they are not the same.

dinner

Dinner is the main meal of the day.

dinosaur

A **dinosaur** is a huge animal that lived millions of years ago. There are no more living dinosaurs.

dirty

When something is **dirty**, it is not clean. The dirty shoe is the one that is covered in mud.

disguise

A **disguise** is something you wear to hide who you are. Disguises make you look like someone else.

dive

To **dive** is to jump headfirst into water. A **diver** is a person who can dive.

doctor

A **doctor** is a person who helps sick or injured people to get well.

dog

A **dog** is a furry animal with a tail that wags. Dogs are often kept as pets.

doll

A **doll** is a kind of toy. Dolls look like babies or miniature people.

dolphin

A **dolphin** is an animal that lives in the sea. Dolphins are friendly and intelligent animals.

donkey

A **donkey** is an animal that looks like a small horse. Donkeys have long ears and bray (cry out) loudly.

door

A **door** covers an entrance and can be opened and closed.

double

When something is **double**, it is twice as big or twice as many.

down

To move **down** is to go to a lower place. This train is travelling across the bridge and down the slope.

dragon

A **dragon** is an imaginary animal. Dragons have wings, and they breathe fire.

dragonfly

A **dragonfly** is a flying insect with a long, thin body and four wings.

draw

To **draw** is to make lines that form a picture.

drawer

A **drawer** is a box that slides in and out of a **chest of drawers** or other piece of furniture.

dress

A **dress** is a piece of clothing worn by girls and **women.** The top and the skirt are joined together to make one piece.

dress

To **dress** yourself is to put on your clothes.

drill

A **drill** is a tool for making holes in wood, stone, or metal.

drink

To **drink** is to swallow a liquid, such as juice or water.

drive

To **drive** a vehicle is to operate and steer it. A **driver** is a person who can drive a vehicle.

drop

To **drop** something is to let it fall to the ground.

drum

A **drum** is a musical instrument that you play by hitting it with **drumsticks**.

dry

When you **dry** something, you stop it from being wet. This boy is drying a wet plate.

duck

drake

duck

duckling

A **duck** is a water bird. Ducks have webbed **feet** and a flat bill. A male duck is called a **drake** and a baby duck is called a **duckling**.

dump truck

A **dump truck** is a truck that is used to carry heavy loads of sand, **soil**, or stones. Its back lifts up so the load can be dumped out easily.

E e

eagle

An **eagle** is a large, powerful bird of prey.

ear

Your **ears** are part of your head. You have two ears for hearing.

Earth

Earth is the planet where we live. The Earth is our world.

easel

An **easel** is a stand for holding a picture.

eat

To **eat** is to put food into your mouth, chew it, and swallow it.

egg

An **egg** is an unborn baby animal. Birds, insects, fish, and reptiles lay eggs. When an egg hatches, a baby animal comes out.

eight

Eight is the number that comes after seven and before nine.

elbow

Your **elbow** is the middle joint in your arm.

elbow

electricity

Electricity is a powerful force. Electricity makes machines work, and gives us light and heat.

elephant

An **elephant** is a huge, grey animal with a long trunk, large floppy ears, and two tusks.

empty

Something that is **empty** has nothing in it.

emu

An **emu** is a large Australian bird with long legs. Emus cannot fly, but they can run very fast.

engine

An **engine** is a machine that makes things move or run. All cars have engines.

engineer

An **engineer** is someone who builds and mends engines and machinery. Some engineers build bridges and buildings.

enter

To **enter** a building is to go into it through an **entrance**.

envelope

An **envelope** is a paper covering for a **letter**.

equal

When things are **equal**, they are the same size, number, or weight as each other. These scales show that the red apples and green apples are equal in weight.

equator

The **equator** is an imaginary line around the Earth, halfway between the **North Pole** and the **South Pole**.

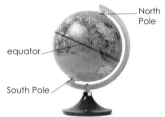

North Pole

equator

South Pole

escalator

An **escalator** is a moving staircase.

exercise

To **exercise** is to make your body stronger and fitter. This boy is exercising.

exit

EXIT

The **exit** is the way out of a building.

expensive

When something is **expensive**, it costs a lot of money to buy.

£30.00

£2.00

explode

When something **explodes**, it blows up and makes a loud noise.

eye

Your **eyes** are part of your face. You have two eyes for seeing.

F f

face

Your **face** is the front part of your head. Your eyes, nose, and mouth are parts of your face.

eyebrow
eye
mouth
forehead
nose

factory

A **factory** is a building where people work together and use machines to make something.

fair

A **fair** is a place where people go to have fun. You can ride on a merry-go-round or a big wheel, and play games to win prizes.

fall

To **fall** is to drop to the ground.

family

A **family** is a group of people who are related to each other. A **mother**, a **father**, a **brother**, and a **sister** are just one kind of family.

fan

A **fan** is a folded piece of paper, silk, or plastic that you wave to make a breeze.

farm

A **farm** is a piece of land for growing crops and keeping animals. A **farmer** is a person who works on a farm.

fast

When something moves **fast** it moves very quickly. This top is spinning fast.

fat

When something is **fat** it is not thin. One of these hamsters looks fat because its cheeks are packed with nuts.

feather

A **feather** is one of the soft, light parts that covers a bird's body.

fight

To **fight** is to battle against someone or something.

film

Film is a thin strip of material that can store images and sounds. It was often used to make photographs, or films for the **cinema**, but today using **digital** images is more common.

finger

Your **finger** is a part of your hand. You have ten fingers.

fingerprint

A **fingerprint** is the mark made when you press your finger on something.

finish

To **finish** is to reach the end of something.

fire

A **fire** is heat, flames, and light made by something burning.

fire engine

A **fire engine** is a large truck that carries **firefighters,** hoses, and a water pump to a fire.

first aid

First aid is the help given to an injured person before a doctor arrives.

fish

A **fish** is an animal that lives in water.

fish

To **fish** is to try to catch a fish.

five

Five is the number that comes after four and before six.

flag

A **flag** is a symbol of a country, a club, or a group of people. It is made from a large piece of **cloth** with a pattern on it.

flipper

A **flipper** is a kind of arm on an animal such as a sea lion or a penguin. Flippers are used for swimming or moving around on land.

flipper

float

When something **floats,** it stays on top of water or another liquid.

flood

A **flood** is a great flow of water that goes over dry land.

flour

Flour is a powder made from grain. It is used to make bread and cakes.

flower

A **flower** is the colourful part of a plant or a tree. There are many different kinds of flowers.

flute

A **flute** is a long, thin musical instrument. You play a flute by blowing across a hole at one end and pressing the keys with your fingers.

fly

To **fly** is to move through the air like an aeroplane, a kite, a bird, or a flying insect.

fly

A **fly** is a small, flying insect with two wings and six legs.

fog

Fog is a thick, grey cloud that hangs close to the ground.

fold

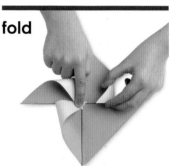

To **fold** something is to bend one part over the other part.

food

Food is all the things that we eat. Food gives us energy and helps our bodies to grow bigger and stronger.

foot

Your **foot** is the part of your body at the end of your leg. You have two **feet.**

football

American football

A **football** is a round or oval ball used to play the team games of **football** or **American football.**

footprint

A **footprint** is the mark made by your shoe or foot on the ground.

forest

A **forest** is a large area of land where lots of trees grow.

fork

A **fork** is a tool that you use to pick up food.

fossil

A **fossil** is the remains of an animal or plant that lived millions of years ago. Fossils are found in rocks.

fountain

A **fountain** is a jet of water that shoots up into the air.

four

Four is the number that comes after three and before five.

fox

A **fox** is a wild animal that looks like a dog with a long, bushy tail.

friend

A **friend** is someone who you like a lot.

frog

A **frog** is an animal that lives in and around water. Frogs have strong back legs for jumping.

fruit

Fruit is the juicy, seeded part of a plant. We eat fruit.

frying pan

A **frying pan** is a wide, flat, metal cooking dish with a handle.

full

When something is **full** it can hold no more.

fur

Fur is the thick, soft hair that grows on the skin of some animals and keeps them warm.

furniture

cupboard

table

sofa

chair

bed

Pieces of **furniture** are large movable objects in a house, an office, or a shop. Chairs and tables are pieces of furniture.

G g

game

People play many different types of games. Each **game** has its own rules.

garage

A **garage** is a covered place where cars are parked.

garden

A **garden** is a place where colourful flowers, vegetables, or other plants are grown.

gate

A **gate** is a door in a fence or a wall.

ghost

A **ghost** is a dead person who some people think they can see, but many people think ghosts are make-believe.

giant

A **giant** is a huge, imaginary person.

giraffe

A **giraffe** is an animal with a very long neck and long, thin legs. Giraffes are the tallest animals in the world.

girl

A **girl** is a **female** child.

give

To **give** is to hand something to someone.

glass

Glass is a hard material that you can see through. It breaks easily.

glasses

Glasses are worn over your eyes if you need help to see better.

globe

A **globe** is a round ball with a map of the world printed on it.

glove

A **glove** is a warm covering for your hand.

glue

Glue is a liquid or paste that you use to stick things together.

goal

A **goal** is two posts with a net or an empty space between them. In some games, you kick a ball between the posts to score a goal.

goat

A **goat** is an animal with a beard under its chin and short horns. A female goat is called a **nanny goat**, a male goat is called a **billy goat**, and a young goat is called a **kid.**

nanny goat

kid

goggles

Goggles are special glasses that protect your eyes in the water.

gold

Gold is a precious yellow metal that can be made into **jewellery.** Gold is found in rocks.

goldfish

A **goldfish** is a small orange fish that is often kept as a pet.

golf

Golf is an outdoor game that is played with golf clubs and a golf ball. You use a club to hit a ball into a series of holes in the ground.

goose

A **goose** is a water bird with a short bill and a long neck. Male **geese** are called **ganders** and young geese are called **goslings.**

gander

gosling

gorilla

A **gorilla** is a big, strong ape.

grandparent

A **grandparent** is the parent of your mother or your father. Here are a **grandmother**, a **grandfather**, and their **grandchildren.**

grape

A **grape** is a small, round fruit that grows in a bunch on a grapevine.

grapefruit

A **grapefruit** is a round, juicy fruit with a yellow skin.

grass

Grass is a green plant that covers the ground.

grasshopper

A **grasshopper** is a jumping insect with long, strong legs.

green

Green is a colour. Many plants are green.

grow

To **grow** is to get bigger.

guitar

A **guitar** is a musical instrument with strings and a long neck. You play a guitar by strumming or plucking the strings.

gymnast

A **gymnast** is a person who does special exercises. Gymnasts train in a **gymnasium.**

H h

hair

Hair is the soft covering that grows on your head and body.

half

A **half** is one of two equal parts. Two **halves** make a whole.

hammer

A **hammer** is a tool that you use to knock in nails.

hand

Your **hand** is the part of your body below your wrist at the end of your arm. You hold things in your hands.

handle

A **handle** is the part of something that you hold.

hang

To **hang** something is to attach the top of it to a hook.

hangar

A **hangar** is a large building where aeroplanes are kept.

happy

A **happy** person is someone who feels pleased.

harbour

A **harbour** is a sheltered place on a coast where ships and boats are kept safely.

hat

A **hat** is a covering for your head.

hawk

A **hawk** is a bird of prey. Hawks eat small animals, such as rabbits and fish.

head

Your **head** is the part of your body that is above your neck.

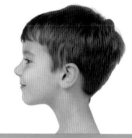

headlamp

A **headlamp** is a light on the front of a vehicle.

hearing aid

A **hearing aid** is a machine that you wear in your ear if you need help to hear things.

heart

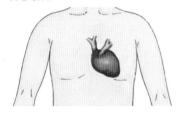

Your **heart** is inside your chest. It pumps blood around your body.

heavy

If something is **heavy**, it weighs a lot and is difficult to move.

heel

Your **heel** is at the back of your foot.

helicopter

A **helicopter** is a flying machine that has long blades on top that spin around to make it hover in the air.

helmet

A **helmet** is a hard hat that protects your head.

help

To **help** someone is to make their job easier.

hibernate

When an animal **hibernates**, it sleeps through the cold, winter months. Animals that hibernate include dormice and hedgehogs.

hide

To **hide** is to put something in a place where no one can see it. This boy is hiding himself behind the sofa.

high

When something is **high**, it is not low. These hot-air balloons are high in the sky.

hill

A **hill** is a big hump in the land. Hills are smaller than mountains.

hip

Your **hip** is the bony part of your body that sticks out just below your **waist.** Your legs join your body at your hips.

hippopotamus

A **hippopotamus** is a large animal with very thick skin and short legs. It likes to wallow in water.

hold

To **hold** something is to have it in your hands or arms.

hole

A **hole** is an opening in something.

honey

Honey is a sweet, thick, sticky liquid that is made by bees.

hoof

A **hoof** is the hard covering on the **feet** of some animals.

hop

To **hop** is to jump up and down on one leg.

horn

A **horn** is something that makes a loud noise to warn people of danger.

horse

A **horse** is a large animal with a mane, a tail, and hooves. A female horse is called a **mare**, a male horse is called a **stallion**, and a baby horse is called a **foal**.

hospital

A **hospital** is a place where doctors and nurses take care of sick or injured people.

hot

When something is **hot**, it is not cold. This cup of coffee is very hot.

hotel

A **hotel** is a building with lots of bedrooms. People pay to stay in hotels. Many hotels have restaurants.

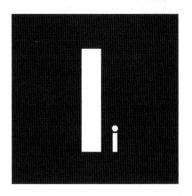

house

A **house** is a building where people live.

hug

To **hug** something is to put your arms around it and hold it tightly.

hutch

A **hutch** is a pet rabbit's house.

hyena

A **hyena** is a wild animal that looks a bit like a dog. Its call sounds like a loud, human laugh.

ice

Ice is frozen water.

iceberg

An **iceberg** is a very large piece of ice that floats in the ocean.

hundred

A **hundred** is the number that comes after 99 and before 101.

ice cream

Ice cream is a frozen dessert made from cream or custard.

icicle

An **icicle** is a hanging piece of ice made by water freezing as it drips.

igloo

An **igloo** is a house made from blocks of snow and ice.

iguana

An **iguana** is a large lizard with a long tail and a ridge of spines along its back. Some iguanas live in trees.

injection

An **injection** is a way that a doctor or a nurse can give you a vaccine or a medicine. A hollow needle is pricked into your skin, and the vaccine or medicine is pushed through the needle into your body.

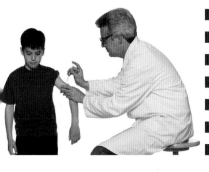

injure

To **injure** yourself is to hurt yourself. This girl has injured her leg.

insect

An **insect** is a tiny animal with six legs. Most insects have wings.

inside

When something is **inside**, it is within and not outside. These shoes are inside a shoebox.

instrument

An **instrument** is something that makes musical sounds.

saxophone

Internet

The **Internet** is a computer network that shares information and connects people all over the world.

invent

To **invent** is to make something that did not exist before. An **inventor** invents things.

invite

To **invite** someone is to ask them to a party or another event. An **invitation** is a card you can send that invites someone to an event.

Please come to my party!

iron

An **iron** is a tool that becomes hot when you switch it on. It is used to take creases out of clothes.

island

An **island** is an area of land with water all around it.

ivy

Ivy is a plant that climbs up walls and trees.

J j

jacket

A **jacket** is a short coat.

jaguar

A **jaguar** is a large, wild cat with a spotty coat.

jam

Jam is a sweet food that you can spread on bread. It is made by boiling fruit with sugar.

jar

A **jar** is a glass container with a wide neck and a lid.

jaw

Your **jaw** is the bony part of your mouth that holds your **teeth.** You move your lower jaw when you chew.

jeans

Jeans are **trousers** made out of strong, cotton **cloth.**

jellyfish

A **jellyfish** is a sea animal that has a soft body and long tentacles.

jewel

emerald

A **jewel** is a precious stone, such as an **emerald** or a **ruby**. Jewels are used to make sparkling **jewellery**.

jigsaw puzzle

A **jigsaw puzzle** is a picture cut up into pieces that you have to fit together again.

judo

Judo is a fighting sport using holds and throws.

jug

A **jug** is a container with a handle and a spout for pouring liquids.

juggle

To **juggle** is to keep several objects in the air by throwing and catching them quickly. A **juggler** is a person who can juggle.

juice

Juice is the liquid that comes out of fruit.

jump

To **jump** is to leap into the air so that both your **feet** leave the ground.

jungle

A **jungle** is a hot, steamy forest where it rains a lot. There are many very tall trees in a jungle. Jungles can also be called **rainforests**.

K k

kangaroo

A **kangaroo** is an animal with long, powerful back legs, which it uses for jumping. A female kangaroo carries her baby in her pouch.

karate

Karate is a fighting sport using kicks and hand chops.

kennel

A **kennel** is a house for a pet dog.

key

A **key** is a tool that you use to lock or unlock a door.

kick

To **kick** is to hit out with your foot.

king

A **king** is a man who heads a country. Kings live in palaces.

kiss

To **kiss** is to touch someone with your lips.

kitchen

A **kitchen** is a room where food is cooked and meals are made.

kite

A **kite** is a toy that you fly in the wind.

kitten

A **kitten** is a young cat.

knee

Your **knee** is the joint in the middle of your leg. Your leg bends at your knee.

kneel

To **kneel** is to go down on your knees.

knife

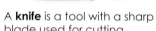

A **knife** is a tool with a sharp blade used for cutting.

knight

Knights were brave soldiers who lived a long time ago. They rode horses and wore armour.

knit

To **knit** is to join loops of wool to make clothes and other things. You knit with knitting needles.

knock

To **knock** is to tap something with your knuckles to make a noise.

knot

A **knot** is a fastening made by tying things together. This is a knot in a piece of rope.

koala

A **koala** is a grey, furry animal with big ears and a black nose. Koalas eat eucalyptus leaves and live in trees.

L l

laboratory

A **laboratory** is a place where people learn about science and do experiments.

ladder

A **ladder** is a tall climbing frame with lots of steps. You climb ladders to reach high places.

ladybird

A **ladybird** is a tiny insect that often has spotty wing cases.

lake

A **lake** is a large area of water surrounded by land.

lamb

A **lamb** is a young sheep.

lamp

A **lamp** gives off light. Lamps have light bulbs, and many also have lampshades.

large

When something is **large,** it is not small. The large doll can contain all the smaller dolls.

laugh

To **laugh** is to make sounds that show you are happy.

lawn

A **lawn** is an area of ground that is covered with grass. A lawn is cut with a **lawnmower.**

leaf

A **leaf** is a flat, green part of a plant that grows from a stem.

land

Land is the part of the Earth that is not water. We live on land.

lean

To **lean** is to tilt your body to one side.

left

Left is the opposite of right. This girl is about to make a left turn on her bicycle.

leg

Your **leg** is the part of your body between your bottom and your foot. People walk on two legs.

lemon

A **lemon** is a yellow fruit with a very sour taste.

leopard

A **leopard** is a wild cat that has sharp **teeth** and claws. Leopards have a light yellow coat with black spots.

letter

A **letter** is part of an alphabet. You put letters together to make words.

lettuce

Lettuce is a leafy, green vegetable that you eat in a salad.

library

A **library** is a place where lots of books are kept on shelves for people to read. You can borrow books from most libraries.

lick

To **lick** something is to touch it with your tongue.

lifeboat

A **lifeboat** is a boat that is used to rescue people out at sea.

lift

To **lift** something is to pick it up. This boy is lifting a bucket.

light

If something is **light,** it is not heavy. Light things weigh very little and are easy to lift.

lighthouse

A **lighthouse** is a tall tower on the coast with a bright light on the top. Lighthouses guide ships around dangerous coasts.

lightning

Lightning is a flash of light that appears in the sky during a **thunderstorm.**

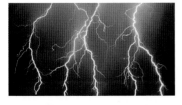

lion

A **lion** is a big, fierce, wild cat that roars. A male lion has a shaggy **mane** around its head. A female lion is called a **lioness.**

lioness

mane

lion

lip

Your **lips** are the soft, fleshy edges of your mouth.

liquid

A **liquid** is wet and can be poured. Orange juice is a liquid.

litter

Litter is the rubbish that should be recycled or put in a rubbish bin.

little

When something is **little,** it is not large. The purple flower is little.

lizard

A **lizard** is a reptile with a long, scaly body, a tail, and four short legs.

lobster

A **lobster** is a sea animal with a hard shell, ten legs, and large claws on its front legs.

lock

A **lock** is a fastening that you open with a key. This is a **padlock** and key.

key

padlock

log

A **log** is a thick piece of wood cut from a tree **trunk.**

long

When something is **long**, it is not short. One of these strings of beads is long and the other is short.

low

When something is **low**, it is not high. This girl is low down in the grass.

M m

look

To **look** is to use your eyes to see things.

luggage

Luggage is all the bags and suitcases that you take on holiday.

machine

A **machine** is an object with parts that work together to perform a task. Clocks, cars, bicycles, and computers are all machines.

lose

When you **lose** something, you cannot find it. This girl has lost a shoe.

lunch

Lunch is the meal that you eat in the middle of the day.

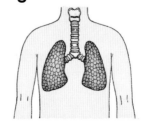

magazine

A **magazine** is a collection of pages with text and pictures, usually about a certain subject, printed every week or month.

love

To **love** is to like someone or something very much.

lung

Your **lungs** are inside your chest. You have two lungs for breathing.

magic

Magic is a way of doing amazing tricks that seem to be impossible. A **magician** is a person who can do magic tricks.

magnet

A **magnet** is a piece of **iron** or **steel** metal that can pull other pieces of iron or steel towards it.

magnifying glass

A **magnifying glass** is a special piece of glass that makes things look bigger than they really are.

mammal

A **mammal** is a warm-blooded animal that feeds on its mother's milk.

man

A **man** is a grown-up boy.

map

A **map** is a drawing of an area as seen from above. This map of the world shows where all the countries are.

market

A **market** is a place where people buy and sell things.

mask

A **mask** is a covering for your face. You wear a mask to disguise yourself.

match

A **match** is a stick with a tip that creates a flame when you rub it on a rough surface.

mathematics

Mathematics is the study of numbers, shapes, and sizes.

meal

A **meal** is the food that you eat at one time.

measure

To **measure** something is to find out what size it is.

meat

Meat is the part of an animal that is eaten as food.

mechanic

A **mechanic** is a person who repairs cars or other machines.

microscope

A **microscope** is an instrument that makes tiny things look bigger.

microwave oven

A **microwave oven** is a machine that cooks food very quickly.

medal

A **medal** is a piece of stamped metal, often round, that is given to a person who wins a competition.

melt

When something **melts**, it turns to liquid as it warms up.

metal

Metal is a hard material, such as **copper, iron,** or gold, that is found in rocks and used to make things.

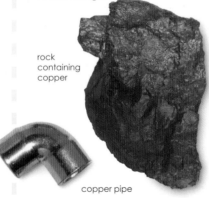

rock containing copper

copper pipe

medicine

Medicine is a liquid or a pill that you swallow to make you better if you are ill.

midday

Midday is the middle of the day. You eat your lunch at midday.

meet

To **meet** someone is to come face to face with them.

microphone

A **microphone** is a machine that makes your voice sound louder.

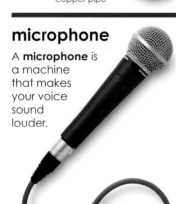

midnight

Midnight is the middle of the night. You are asleep at midnight.

milk

Milk is a white liquid that some animals make to feed their babies. Many people drink cow's milk.

mine

A **mine** is a deep hole under the ground where people dig for rocks, such as coal.

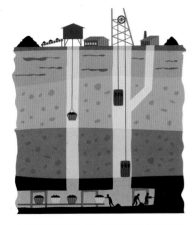

mineral

Minerals can be found in rocks, and are dug out of mines.

mirror

A **mirror** is a special piece of glass in which you can see your reflection.

mix

To **mix** things is to stir them together.

money

Money is the coins and paper notes that we use to buy things.

monkey

Monkeys are furry animals with long arms and long legs. Most monkeys also have long tails for swinging in trees.

monster

A **monster** is a make-believe creature that looks strange and frightening. You can read about monsters in fairy tales.

month

A **month** is a measure of time that is about 30 days long. There are 12 months in a year.

JANUARY
FEBRUARY
MARCH
APRIL
MAY
JUNE
JULY
AUGUST
SEPTEMBER
OCTOBER
NOVEMBER
DECEMBER

moon

The **moon** is the Earth's satellite. It shines in the sky at night.

moose

A **moose** is a large deer. Moose have long faces, and male moose have huge **antlers**.

mosque

A **mosque** is a building where Muslim people meet to pray.

mosquito

A **mosquito** is a flying insect that bites your skin to feed on your blood.

moth

A **moth** is an insect that looks like a butterfly. It flies around at night.

motorbike

A **motorbike** is a vehicle that you ride. It has two wheels and an engine.

mountain

A **mountain** is a very high, large, rocky hill.

mouse

A **mouse** is a small, furry animal with a long tail. **Mice** live in nests.

mouse

A **mouse** is a small machine that you can use to move the pointer on a computer **screen.**

mouth

Your **mouth** is part of your face. You use your mouth for eating and speaking.

mud

Mud is wet, soft earth.

muscle

Muscles are part of your body. They give you strength to move your body, and to lift things.

museum

A **museum** is a building where you can see works of art and things from long ago.

mushroom

A **mushroom** is a fungus that is shaped like a small umbrella. You can eat some mushrooms, but others are poisonous.

music

Music is the notes that you read, or the sound that you make, when you are singing or playing a musical instrument.

musician

A **musician** is a person who can make music by playing a musical instrument.

N n

nail

A **nail** is a thin piece of metal with a sharp point at one end. You hammer nails into wood.

narrow

When something is **narrow**, it is not wide. Narrow spaces are difficult to squeeze through.

navy

A **navy** is a large group of warships carrying sailors who are trained to fight at sea in times of war.

neck

Your **neck** is the part of your body that is between your head and your shoulders.

needle

A **needle** is a thin, pointed piece of metal with a hole. You use it for sewing.

nest

A **nest** is a home some animals make, where they live and care for their babies.

net

Net is material made from knotted string or thread. You can catch fish in a **fishing net.**

new

When something is **new**, it is not old. New things have just been made or bought.

newspaper

A **newspaper** is a collection of printed sheets of paper. You read newspapers to find out what is happening in your area or around the world.

newt

A **newt** is an animal that lives in and around water.

night

Night is the time when it is dark outside. Night begins at sunset and ends at sunrise.

nine

Nine is the number that comes after eight and before ten.

noise

A **noise** is a loud sound. The girl is making a noise on her tuba.

nose

Your **nose** is part of your face. You breathe and smell through your nose.

number

A **number** is a symbol that tells you how many things there are.

0 1 2 3 4 5

nurse

A **nurse** is a person who is trained to take care of sick or injured people.

nut

A **nut** is a small piece of metal that you screw onto a **bolt**. Nuts and bolts are used to hold things together.

nut

bolt

nut

A **nut** is a fruit or a seed with a hard shell.

nutcracker

A **nutcracker** is a tool that you use to break open nuts.

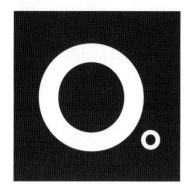

office

An **office** is a place where people go to work. There are desks, chairs, and computers in offices.

oar

An **oar** is a long pole with a flat blade at one end. You use oars to row a boat.

ocean

An **ocean** is a large body of salt water. The Pacific and the Atlantic are oceans.

oil

Oil is a greasy liquid. It helps some machines to run smoothly.

old

When something is **old**, it is not new. Old things look used.

onion

An **onion** is a round vegetable that often makes your eyes water when it is cut open.

open

When something is **open**, it is not shut or closed.

octopus

An **octopus** is a sea animal with eight long arms and a soft, round body.

one

One is the number that comes after zero and before two. When we count, we start with one.

opera

An **opera** is a play in which the words are sung to music.

53

opposite

When things are the **opposite** of each other, they are completely different. Hot and cold are opposites, so are front and back.

optician

An **optician** is a person who helps people to buy the right glasses for their eyes.

orange

Orange is a colour. It can be made by mixing red and yellow.

orange

An **orange** is a round, juicy fruit with a thick, orange-coloured skin.

orang-utan

An **orang-utan** is a large ape with long fur and strong arms.

orchard

An **orchard** is an area of land where fruit trees are grown.

orchestra

An **orchestra** is a large group of musicians playing instruments together.

organ

An **organ** is a musical instrument with a keyboard, and long, metal pipes that make sounds when air is pushed through them.

ostrich

An **ostrich** is a large bird from Africa with a long neck, long legs, and big feathers. Ostriches cannot fly, but they can run very fast.

otter

An **otter** is a furry animal that lives in and around water.

outside

When something is **outside**, it is not inside. This puppy is outside its kennel.

oval

An **oval** is a shape. Eggs are oval.

oven

An **oven** is a machine that cooks food.

owl

An **owl** is a bird with a large head and big, round eyes. Most owls hunt for food at night.

oyster

An **oyster** is a sea animal with a soft body that is protected by two hard shells. Some oysters make pearls inside their shells.

P p

page

A **page** is one side of a sheet of paper in a book.

paint

To **paint** is to colour something with paint. You can paint a picture.

paint

Paint is a coloured liquid that is used for painting things.

pair

A **pair** is a set of two things that are used together, such as these socks.

palace

A **palace** is a very large, grand house where people such as kings and queens live.

palm

Your **palm** is the inner surface of your hand.

palm tree

A **palm tree** is a tree that grows in hot places. Palm trees have large leaves that grow at the top of a long trunk.

panda

A **panda** is a large, furry animal. Giant pandas look like bears with black-and-white fur.

panther

A **panther** is a large leopard with a black coat.

paper

Paper is a material you use to write on.

parachute

A **parachute** is a large piece of material that is shaped like an umbrella. Parachutes help people to float through the air and land safely on the ground.

parcel

A **parcel** is something wrapped in paper. We post parcels, and we give them as presents.

parent

A **parent** is a person who has a child. Your mother and father are your parents. You are their **son** or **daughter.**

park

A **park** is an area of land where people can enjoy the open space and playgrounds.

parrot

A **parrot** is a bird with brightly coloured feathers. Some parrots can be trained to repeat words.

party

A **party** is an event where a group of people come together to celebrate. You might have a party on your birthday.

passenger

A **passenger** is a person who travels in a vehicle. Passengers don't drive.

path

A **path** is a track for people to walk on.

patient

A **patient** is a person who is ill and being cared for by a nurse or a doctor.

paw

A **paw** is the foot of some animals.

pay

To **pay** for something is to give money for it.

pea

A **pea** is a small, round, green vegetable that grows in a pod.

peach

A **peach** is a sweet, juicy fruit with a soft skin, and a stone in the middle.

peacock

A **peacock** is a bird with colourful tail feathers that open out like a fan.

peanut

A **peanut** is a seed that grows in a pod in the soil.

pear

A **pear** is a fruit that narrows at the top and has pips in the middle.

pearl

A **pearl** is a small, white gemstone that is found in some oyster shells. Pearls are used to make **jewellery**.

pebble

A **pebble** is a small, smooth stone found on the beach.

peel

Peel is the skin of some fruits and vegetables.

peel

To **peel** a fruit or a vegetable is to take the skin off it. This boy is peeling a banana.

pelican

A **pelican** is a bird that has a large beak with a pouch, which it uses to catch fish to eat.

pen

A **pen** is a tool filled with ink. You use a pen for writing.

pencil

A **pencil** is a tool you write or draw with. It is made of wood and graphite.

penguin

A **penguin** is a black-and-white sea bird that cannot fly. Penguins use their wings (also called flippers) to swim in the water.

people

People are **men**, **women**, and **children**.

pepper

Pepper is a strong spice that is often ground up to flavour food.

perfume

Perfume is a sweet-smelling liquid made from flower petals and spices. You put perfume on your body.

pet

A **pet** is a tame animal that you take care of and keep at home.

petal

A **petal** is a part of a flower. It is often brightly coloured.

photograph

A **photograph** is a picture taken with a camera.

photographer

A **photographer** is a person who takes photographs.

piano

A **piano** is a large musical instrument with black and white keys. You press the keys to make music.

picnic

A **picnic** is a meal that you eat outside.

picture

When you create a **picture**, you draw or paint what something looks like.

pie

A **pie** is a pastry case filled with fruit, meat, or vegetables, and baked in an oven.

pig

A **pig** is an animal with a snout for a nose, a little tail, big ears, and bristly hair on its skin. A male pig is called a **boar,** a female pig is called a **sow,** and a baby pig is called a **piglet.**

pigeon

A **pigeon** is a bird with a plump body and a small head. Most pigeons live in cities.

pile

A **pile** is a lot of things stacked on top of one another.

pillow

A **pillow** is a bag of soft material for your head to rest on.

pilot

A **pilot** is a person who flies an aeroplane.

pin

A **pin** is a thin, pointed piece of metal used to hold **cloth** together.

pineapple

A **pineapple** is a large fruit with rough, bumpy skin and pointed leaves. The fruit inside is sweet and juicy.

pink

Pink is a colour. It can be made by mixing red and white.

pipe

A **pipe** is a hollow tube of metal or plastic. Liquid runs through pipes.

pirate

A **pirate** is a robber who attacks ships at sea and steals from them.

planet

A **planet** is a huge, round mass, mostly made up of rock and metal, or gas, that moves around the sun or another star. Eight planets move around the sun.

Jupiter Uranus Neptune Saturn Mars Earth Mercury Venus

plant

A **plant** is anything that grows in the **soil**. Flowers and trees are plants.

plastic

Plastic is a material made from chemicals. This blow-up toy is made out of plastic.

plate

A **plate** is a flat dish that you put food on.

play

To **play** is to do something for fun.

plum

A **plum** is a sweet fruit with a stone in the middle.

plumber

A **plumber** is a person who works on water and gas pipes.

pocket

A **pocket** is a small bag that is sewn into your clothes.

point

A **point** is the sharp end of something. These objects all have points.

polar bear

A **polar bear** is a huge bear covered in thick, white fur.

police officer

A **police officer** is a person who protects people and makes sure laws are obeyed.

polish

To **polish** is to rub something to make it shine.

pond

A **pond** is a small lake.

pony

A **pony** is a small horse.

poppy

A **poppy** is a flower with big petals. Poppies can be many different colours, including red, orange, and yellow.

porcupine

A **porcupine** is an animal with large, pointed hairs called quills.

postcard

A **postcard** is a card that you can send in the post without an envelope. It usually has a picture on one side, and space for a message, an address, and a stamp on the other side.

post office

A **post office** is a place where you can buy stamps, and post letters and parcels. The letters and parcels are sorted in a **sorting office**.

post office   sorting office

potato

A **potato** is a hard vegetable that grows in the ground.

pour

To **pour** a liquid is to tip it out of a container.

present

A **present** is something that you give to someone. We often give presents on special occasions, such as birthdays.

price

The **price** of something is the amount of money you have to pay for it.

£10.50

prickle

A **prickle** is a spike on a plant. This chestnut has prickles.

prince

A **prince** is the son of a king and queen. A **princess** is the daughter of a king and queen.

prize

A **prize** is a reward you may be given if you win a competition.

propeller

A **propeller** is like a fan. It spins round to make boats and aircraft move.

puddle

A **puddle** is a small pool of water.

pull

To **pull** is to take hold of something and move it towards you.

pump

A **pump** is a machine that forces liquid or gas into or out of something. This pump forces air into a bicycle tyre.

bicycle pump

air hose

puncture

A **puncture** is a small hole in something, made by a sharp object. A puncture in a tyre lets the air out.

pupa

A **pupa** is a caterpillar while it is in a cocoon changing into a butterfly or a moth.

puppet

A **puppet** is a doll that is moved by strings or your fingers.

puppy

A **puppy** is a young dog.

purple

Purple is a colour. It can be made by mixing blue and red.

push

To **push** is to take hold of something and move it away from you.

puzzle

A **puzzle** is a game or a problem that you enjoy trying to work out.

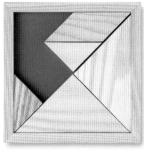

pyramid

A **pyramid** is a building with a square base and sloping, triangular sides. People who lived long ago built pyramids.

python

A **python** is a large snake that kills its prey by squeezing it to death.

quarry

A **quarry** is a place where stone is cut out of the ground. The stone is used to make buildings and other things.

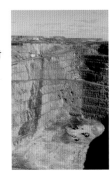

quarter

A **quarter** is one of four equal parts. Four quarters make a whole.

queen

A **queen** is a woman who heads a country. Queens live in palaces.

quick

To be **quick** is to do something in a short time.

quiet

To be **quiet** is to make very little noise or no noise at all.

quilt

A **quilt** is a warm, soft cover for a bed.

quiz

A **quiz** is a game or a test where people try to answer questions.

R r

rabbit

A **rabbit** is a furry, burrowing animal with long ears.

race

A **race** is a competition to find out who is the fastest.

racing car

A **racing car** is a car built for car races. Racing cars go very fast around a track.

radio

A **radio** is a machine that receives radio signals (called radio waves) from the air. It turns them into music or voices that you listen to on the radio.

raft

A **raft** is a flat boat, usually made out of logs.

railway

A **railway** is a metal track for trains to run on. The metal track is made from long, **iron** bars called **rails.**

railway station

A **railway station** is a place where you go to buy a train ticket and catch a train.

rain

Rain is drops of water that fall from clouds in the sky.

rainbow

A **rainbow** is an arc of different colours that appears in the sky when the sun shines through rain. Traditionally, rainbows are described as having seven colours: red, orange, yellow, green, blue, **indigo,** and **violet.**

reach

To **reach** for something is to stretch out your hand to take or touch it. This boy is reaching for a jam tart.

read

To **read** is to understand the meaning of written or printed words.

recorder

A **recorder** is a wooden or plastic musical instrument. You play a recorder by blowing into it and covering the holes with your fingers.

rectangle

A **rectangle** is a shape with two long sides, two shorter sides, and four corners.

recycle

To **recycle** is to process things, such as plastic bottles, papers, or cans, so that they can be reused. We recycle to help the environment.

red

Red is a colour. Tomatoes are red.

refrigerator

A **refrigerator** is a machine that keeps food and drinks cool. Food and drinks are stored in a refrigerator.

repair

To **repair** something is to mend it.

reptile

A **reptile** is a cold-blooded animal with a backbone, and scales or bony plates. Reptiles include lizards, snakes, and turtles.

lizard

snake

rescue

To **rescue** something is to save it from danger or harm.

restaurant

A **restaurant** is a place where you can buy and eat a meal.

rhinoceros

A **rhinoceros** is a large, heavy animal with a thick skin. It has one or two horns on the top of its nose.

ribbon

A **ribbon** is a thin strip of material that you use for decoration.

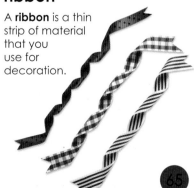

65

rice

Rice is a popular food. It is the seeds of a plant. Rice plants grow in wet ground in hot countries.

ride

To **ride** is to sit on or in something as it moves. This girl is riding a horse.

right

Right is the opposite of left. This girl is making a right turn on her bicycle.

ring

A **ring** is a circle of metal that you wear on your finger.

ring

When something **rings**, it makes a sound. Bells, telephones, and doorbells can all ring.

river

A **river** is a large stream of water that flows into another river, a lake, or the sea.

road

A **road** is a hard track made for cars, trucks, bikes, and other traffic. You travel from one place to another along a road.

robot

A **robot** is a machine that can do some things that people can do. Some robots can do jobs.

rock

A **rock** is a large stone found in the ground or in mountains.

rocket

A **rocket** is a tube-shaped vehicle that flies into space. Hot gases shoot out of the bottom to move it upwards. Rockets put spacecraft into space.

roll

To **roll** is to move along by turning over and over.

roof

A **roof** is the part that covers the top of a building.

room

A **room** is part of a building. A room has a **ceiling**, a **floor**, four **walls**, and a door.

root

A **root** is the part of a plant that grows underground. Roots take up water from the **soil** to feed a plant.

root

rope

Rope is strong, thick string. It can be used to pull or lift things, or to hold things in place.

rose

A **rose** is a flower with a sweet smell and lots of petals. Roses have thorns on their stems.

round

When something is **round**, it is shaped like a circle or a ball.

row

A **row** is a straight line of things.

rug

A **rug** is a piece of material that covers part of a floor.

ruler

A **ruler** is a long, flat, straight tool used for measuring things, or drawing straight lines.

run

To **run** is to move very quickly on your legs.

runway

A **runway** is a strip of hard, flat ground where aircraft can take off and land.

67

S s

sad

A **sad** person is someone who feels unhappy.

saddle

A **saddle** is a **seat** that you put on a horse for the rider to sit on.

sail

A **sail** is a large piece of material attached to a boat. Wind blows into the sail and makes the boat move through the water.

sail

To **sail** is to travel on a boat. A **sailor** is a person who works on or operates a boat. A **sailing boat** is a boat that is moved by wind in its sails.

salad

A **salad** is usually cold, and is a mixture of foods, such as lettuce, tomatoes, and cucumber.

salt

Salt is something found in sea water or underground in rock form. Ground-up salt is used to flavour food.

same

When two things are the **same**, they are like each other in every way.

sand

Sand is grains of rock. It covers a beach or desert.

sandcastles

sandwich

A **sandwich** is two pieces of bread with another food in between them.

satellite

A **satellite** is any object that moves around a planet in space. Mechanical satellites move around the Earth, collecting and sending information.

satellite dish

A **satellite dish** sends information to and receives information from a mechanical satellite.

saucepan

A **saucepan** is a cooking pan with a long handle.

saw

A **saw** is a tool that has a metal blade with sharp **teeth**. You use a saw to cut wood.

scale

A **scale** is a hard, flat, thin covering on a fish or a reptile. This fish is covered with lots of small scales.

scale

A **scale** is a machine that tells you how much things weigh.

scarf

A **scarf** is a strip or a square of fabric worn around your neck.

school

A **school** is a place where you go to learn. At school, your teacher teaches you important things, such as how to read, write, and count.

scientist

A **scientist** is a person who studies a science, such as chemistry.

scissors

Scissors are a tool with two sharp blades. You use scissors to cut things.

scorpion

A **scorpion** is an animal with two large claws and a poisonous sting in its tail.

scratch

To **scratch** yourself is to rub your skin with your fingernails to stop it from itching.

screw

A **screw** is a thin, metal spike with grooves. Screws hold things together.

scrub

To **scrub** something is to rub it with a brush to clean it. The potato is being scrubbed.

sea

The **sea** is the part of the Earth that is salt water. Fish and other sea animals live in the sea.

seagull

A **seagull** is a bird with grey and white feathers. You often see seagulls near the coast.

sea horse

A **sea horse** is a fish with a head that looks like a horse's head, and a long tail.

seal

A **seal** is a large animal that lives in the sea and on land. Seals have fur and whiskers, and flippers that help them to swim.

season

spring

summer

autumn

winter

A **season** is a time of year. There are four seasons and they always follow the same order: **spring, summer, autumn,** and then **winter.**

seat belt

A **seat belt** is a safety strap in a vehicle. You wear a seat belt around your body to hold you in place.

seaweed

Seaweed is a plant that grows in the sea.

seed

A **seed** is the part of a plant that grows into a new plant.

seesaw

A **seesaw** is a balanced plank that two people can ride on. The people sit at each end of the plank and move up and down.

sell

To **sell** something is to give it to someone in return for money.

Lemonade
50p

seven

Seven is the number that comes after six and before eight.

sew

To **sew** is to join material together using a needle and thread.

shadow

A **shadow** is a dark shape that you make when you stand in the way of light.

shake

To **shake** something is to move it quickly up and down or from side to side.

shape

A **shape** is the outside line of something. Circles, squares, triangles, and rectangles are all shapes.

share

To **share** something is to give part of it to another person. This boy is sharing his lunch with a friend.

shark

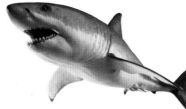

A **shark** is a large sea animal with lots of big, sharp **teeth**.

sharp

When something is **sharp**, it has an edge or a point that can cut things.

sheep

A **sheep** is a farm animal with a thick, woolly coat. A female sheep is called a **ewe** and a male sheep is called a **ram**.

shelf

A **shelf** is a long, flat piece of wood that you keep things on.

shell

A **shell** is the hard, outside covering of an egg, a nut, or an animal.

seashell

ship

A **ship** is a large boat that sails on the sea. Passenger ships carry people.

shirt

A **shirt** is a garment with buttons and sleeves that you wear on the top part of your body.

shoe

A **shoe** is a strong covering for your foot. Shoes protect your **feet.**

shop

A **shop** is a building or part of a building where you can buy things.

short

When something is **short**, it is not long. One set of pencils is short and the other is long.

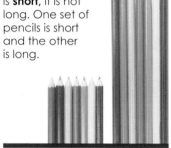

shoulder

Your **shoulder** is the part of your body between your neck and your arm.

shout

To **shout** is to speak very loudly.

shower

A bathroom **shower** sprays water. You stand under the water to wash yourself.

shut

When something is **shut**, it is not open.

sing

To **sing** is to make music with your voice.

sink

When something **sinks**, it goes down below the surface of water or another liquid.

sit

To **sit** is to rest on your bottom on a chair or on the **floor**.

six

Six is the number that comes after five and before seven.

skate

To **skate** is to glide over ice wearing special boots with metal blades called **ice skates**. **Roller skates** and **roller blades** have wheels, so they can roll on the ground.

skeleton

A **skeleton** is all of the bones that make a frame to support the rest of a body.

ski

ski

To **ski** is to slide down snow-covered mountains wearing **skis** on your **feet**.

skip

To **skip** is to jump over a rope. You can also skip along without a rope, hopping from one foot to the other.

skirt

A **skirt** is a garment that hangs down from the **waist**.

sky

The **sky** is above your head where you can see the sun and clouds.

skyscraper

A **skyscraper** is a very tall building that looks as if it is touching the sky.

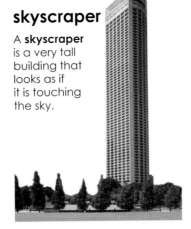

sledge

A **sledge** is a vehicle that is used to carry people over snow.

sleep

To **sleep** is to close your eyes and rest your body and mind. You go to sleep at night or when you are tired.

slice

A **slice** is a thin piece cut from a larger object.

slide

A **slide** is something you slip down. It has a ladder or steps to climb and a slippery slope.

slow

When something is **slow,** it doesn't move very fast, or it takes a long time.

small

When something is **small,** it is little and not big.

smile

A **smile** is what you do with your face to show that you are happy.

snail

A **snail** is an animal with a soft body and a shell on its back.

snake

A **snake** is an animal with a long, thin body, scaly skin, and no legs.

snow

Snow is tiny, white flakes of frozen water. Snow falls from clouds in cold weather.

snowman

A **snowman** is a figure made out of snow.

soap

Soap is something that you use with water to wash things.

soccer

Soccer, or **football**, is a game played by two teams who kick a ball to score goals.

sock

A **sock** is a piece of clothing for your foot.

sofa

A **sofa** is a long, cushioned **seat** with a back and arms. Two or three people can sit on a sofa.

soldier

A **soldier** is a person who is a member of an army.

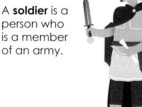

solid

When something is **solid**, it keeps its shape and is firm. Liquids and gases are not solid.

space

Space is the place above the Earth where there is no air. The planets and stars are in space.

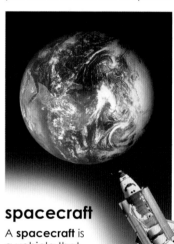

spacecraft

A **spacecraft** is a vehicle that travels in space.

spacesuit

A **spacesuit** is a special suit worn by astronauts that enables them to survive in space.

sparrow

A **sparrow** is a small bird with brown and grey feathers.

spider

A **spider** is an animal with eight legs. Spiders spin **webs** to catch small insects to eat.

spill

To **spill** something is to accidentally knock it out of its container.

spoon

A **spoon** is a tool that you use to pick up food.

sport

A **sport** is a game or a competition played for exercise or fun. There are lots of different sports, such as football, running, and ice hockey.

square

A **square** is a shape with four corners and four equal sides.

squash

To **squash** something is to press it and make it flat.

squeeze

To **squeeze** something is to press both sides of it. This boy is squeezing a **toothpaste** tube.

squirrel

A **squirrel** is a furry animal with a long, bushy tail. Squirrels live in trees and eat nuts.

stable

A **stable** is a building where horses are kept.

stamp

A **stamp** is a small piece of sticky paper that you put on an envelope. A stamp shows that you have paid to post a letter.

stand

To **stand** is to be on your **feet** without moving.

star

A **star** is a bright light in space. You can see lots of stars at night.

starfish

A **starfish** is a sea animal with five or more arms that make the shape of a star.

start

To **start** is to begin something. This girl is starting a race.

steering wheel

A **steering wheel** is the part of a car or truck that you hold to turn the wheels.

stem

stem

A **stem** is the part of a plant from which the flowers and leaves grow.

stone

A **stone** is a small piece of rock.

stopwatch

A **stopwatch** is a special kind of watch that you use to time a race or another activity.

strawberry

A **strawberry** is a small, red, juicy fruit covered with seeds.

stream

A **stream** is a small river.

string

String is a strong, thick thread that you tie round things to hold them in place.

stripe

A **stripe** is a band of colour. All these things have stripes on them.

submarine

A **submarine** is a ship that can travel underwater.

sugar

Sugar is a sweet food made from **sugar cane.** You use sugar to sweeten other foods.

sugar cane

sun

The **sun** is the huge star that gives the Earth heat and light.

sunglasses

Sunglasses are dark glasses that you wear to protect your eyes from strong sunlight.

supermarket

A **supermarket** is a large shop that sells food and things for the house.

swan

A **swan** is a large water bird with a long neck and webbed **feet.**

swim

To **swim** is to move yourself through water using your arms and legs.

swimming pool

A **swimming pool** is where you swim. It is a container of water.

swing

A **swing** is a hanging **seat.** You sit on it and move it backwards and forwards.

sword

A **sword** is a long, sharp, metal blade with a handle at one end.

synagogue

A **synagogue** is a building where Jewish people meet to pray.

table

A **table** is a piece of furniture with a flat top and legs.

tadpole

A **tadpole** is a tiny animal that lives in water. Tadpoles grow into frogs.

tail

A **tail** is the part that sticks out at the back on some animals.

tall

When something is **tall,** it is higher than usual. The girl on the right is taller than her friend.

tambourine

A **tambourine** is a round musical instrument with metal rings. You shake a tambourine to make a sound.

taxi

A **taxi** is a car you hire. You pay the **driver** to take you somewhere.

tea

tea leaves

Tea is a drink made from the dried leaves of a tea plant.

teacher

A **teacher** is a person who helps you to learn things.

team

A **team** is a group of people who work or play together.

tear

A **tear** is a drop of water that comes out of your eye.

tear

To **tear** something is to pull it apart.

telephone

A **telephone** is a machine you use to talk to someone who is far away. A **mobile phone** is a wireless telephone.

mobile phone

telescope

A **telescope** is an instrument that makes faraway objects look bigger and closer.

television

A **television** is a machine that receives messages sent through the air and turns them into sounds and pictures.

temple

A **temple** is a building where people go to pray.

ten

Ten is the number that comes after nine and before eleven.

tennis

Tennis is a game in which two or four players hit a ball with rackets over a net.

tent

A **tent** is a **cloth** or plastic shelter that you use when you camp.

theatre

A **theatre** is a building where you go to see plays, movies, or other performances.

thermometer

A **thermometer** is an instrument that measures how hot or cold something is. You can take your **temperature** with a thermometer.

thigh

Your **thigh** is the part of your leg between your hip and your knee.

thin

When something is **thin**, it is not fat or thick.

thistle

A **thistle** is a prickly plant. It usually has a purple flower.

thorn

A **thorn** is a sharp point on the stem of some plants.

thorn

thread

A **thread** is a strand of cotton you sew with.

three

Three is the number that comes after two and before four.

thumb

Your **thumb** is the widest finger on your hand.

ticket

A **ticket** is a piece of paper or card that shows you have paid, or have to pay, for something.

tie

A **tie** is a narrow strip of cloth you wear knotted around a shirt collar.

tie

To **tie** something is to make a knot or a bow in it to fasten it.

tiger

A **tiger** is a big, fierce, wild cat with an orange-and-black, stripy coat.

tile

A **tile** is a thin, flat covering for **walls** and **floors**.

time

Time is how long things take. It is measured in **hours**, **minutes**, and **seconds**.

tiptoe

To **tiptoe** is to walk on your toes as quietly as you can.

tired

When you feel **tired**, you need to rest or sleep.

toad

A **toad** is an animal that looks like a frog with a dry, rough skin.

toboggan

A **toboggan** is a flat-bottomed sledge that is curved up at the front. You slide down snowy slopes on a toboggan.

toe

Your **toe** is a part of your foot. You have ten toes.

toilet

A **toilet** is where you go to get rid of the waste in your body.

tomato

A **tomato** is a round, red fruit we often eat in salads.

tongue

Your **tongue** is the long, soft part inside your mouth. It helps you to speak, taste, and eat.

tool

A **tool** is something that helps you to do a job. Hammers, pliers, screwdrivers, and wrenches are all tools.

tooth

Your **tooth** is one of the hard, white, bony parts in your mouth. You bite and chew with your **teeth.**

toothbrush

A **toothbrush** is a small brush that you use to clean your **teeth.** You put **toothpaste** on a toothbrush.

top

The **top** of something is the highest part of it. This boy is at the top of the slide.

tornado

A **tornado** is a very strong wind that whirls round and round. Tornados can rip up trees and knock down houses.

toucan

A **toucan** is a black-and-white bird with a large, brightly coloured beak.

tourist

A **tourist** is a person who travels to places of interest, usually on a holiday.

81

towel

A **towel** is a piece of thick **cloth** that you dry yourself with.

town

A **town** is a place with lots of houses, shops, schools, and other buildings.

toy

A **toy** is something that you play with.

tractor

A **tractor** is a farm vehicle that is used to pull heavy machinery.

traffic

Traffic is all the cars, buses, motorbikes, and other vehicles travelling on a road.

train

A **train** is a line of railway carriages that are pulled along a track by an engine. Trains carry people and things from one place to another.

transparent

When something is **transparent**, it is clear, and you can see through it. This glass is transparent.

trapeze

A **trapeze** is a type of swing that is used by acrobats.

tray

A **tray** is a flat board that you use to carry food and drinks. Some trays have handles.

treasure

Treasure is gold, silver, coins, jewels, and other precious things. A **treasure chest** is a box where you keep valuable objects.

tree

A **tree** is a large plant with a thick **trunk**, branches, and leaves.

triangle

A **triangle** is a shape with three straight sides and three corners.

trick

A **trick** is an amazing thing you can do to surprise people. This boy is performing a card trick.

tricycle

A **tricycle** is a vehicle, often for a child, with three wheels that are moved by **pedals.**

trophy

A **trophy** is a large, metal cup that may be given as a prize.

truck

A **truck** is a big, powerful vehicle that is used to carry heavy loads. This truck has a back that lifts up so that its load can fall out easily.

trumpet

A **trumpet** is a brass musical instrument that produces high, clear tones. You blow into the mouthpiece and press the **valves** to make a sound.

valve

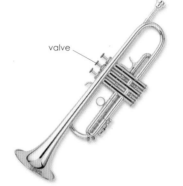

trunk

A **trunk** is an elephant's long nose. Elephants use their trunks to breathe, squirt water into their mouths, and to pick up food.

T-shirt

A **T-shirt** is a collarless top with short sleeves.

tuba

A **tuba** is a large, brass musical instrument with a wide bell. It produces deep, full tones.

bell

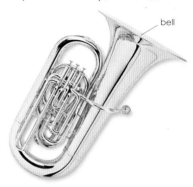

tugboat

A **tugboat** is a small, very powerful boat that is used to pull bigger boats in and out of a harbour.

tugboat

tulip

A **tulip** is a cup-shaped flower that grows from a bulb and blooms in the spring.

tunnel

A **tunnel** is a long passage cut through a hill or under the ground.

turkey

A **turkey** is a large farm bird with long tail feathers and red, floppy skin on its neck.

turtle

A **turtle** is an animal with a bony or leathery shell. Turtles live in water and on land.

tusk

Tusks are the long, pointed **teeth** that some animals have. This elephant has two tusks.

tusk

twig

A **twig** is a small, thin branch of a tree or other woody plant.

twin

A **twin** is one of two **children** that were born at the same time to the same parents.

two

Two is the number that comes after one and before three.

umbrella

An **umbrella** is a piece of waterproof material on a frame that you hold over your head to keep off the rain.

under

To be **under** something is to be below it. The toy soldier is standing under the arch.

underwear

Underwear is clothing that you wear under your other clothes next to your skin. Vests and pants are underwear.

undress

To **undress** is to take off your clothes. You undress to get ready for bed.

unicorn

A **unicorn** is an imaginary animal. It looks like a horse with a long, twisted horn on its **forehead**.

university

A **university** is a place where you can go to learn after leaving school.

up

When something moves **up**, it moves to a higher place. The ball is up in the air.

V v

vacuum cleaner

A **vacuum cleaner** is a machine that sucks up dirt from the floor.

valley

A **valley** is the low land between hills or mountains.

vase

A **vase** is a container for holding cut flowers. You put water in a vase for the flowers to drink.

vegetable

A **vegetable** is a plant with roots, leaves, or stems that you can eat either cooked or raw. Eating a variety of vegetables helps us to stay healthy.

vehicle

A **vehicle** is a machine that carries people and things from one place to another. Cars, trucks, bicycles, trains, and planes are all vehicles.

vet

A **vet** is a doctor for animals. Vets help sick or injured pets, farm animals, or wild animals to get well.

village

A **village** is a small group of houses and other buildings in the countryside.

vine

A **vine** is a climbing plant. Grapes grow on vines planted in **vineyards.**

vinegar

Vinegar is a sour liquid that is used to flavour or preserve food. It is formed when wine, cider, or beer ferments.

violin

A **violin** is a stringed musical instrument made out of wood. You hold it under your chin and draw a **bow** across its strings.

bow

volcano

A **volcano** is a mountain with a hole in the top. Sometimes hot, melted rocks, gases, and ash burst out of a volcano.

vulture

A **vulture** is a large bird that eats dead animals. Many vultures have bald heads.

Ww

wagon

A **wagon** is a cart that is used to carry heavy loads. Wagons are sometimes pulled by horses.

waiter

A **waiter** is a person who serves food and drinks in a restaurant.

walk

To **walk** is to move along on your **feet**, placing one foot on the ground and then the other.

walking stick

A **walking stick** is a long, thin piece of wood that you use to help you walk.

wallaby

A **wallaby** is a furry animal that is like a kangaroo, but usually smaller.

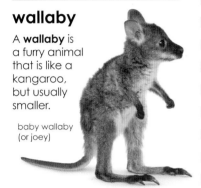

baby wallaby (or joey)

wallet

A **wallet** is a small, flat case that you keep your money in.

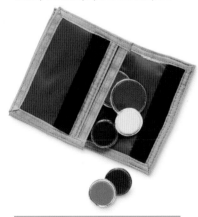

walrus

A **walrus** is a large sea animal with a heavy body and two long tusks.

wash

To **wash** yourself is to clean your body with soap and water.

watch

To **watch** something is to keep your eyes fixed on it.

watch

A **watch** is a small clock that you wear on your wrist so you can tell what the time is.

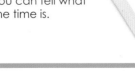

water

Water is the clear liquid that comes out of a tap. We drink water and wash with it. Water falls from the sky as rain.

waterfall

A **waterfall** is a stream or river flowing over the edge of a rock.

water lily

A **water lily** is a flower that grows in ponds and lakes.

watermelon

A **watermelon** is a large fruit with a green skin and a red, watery inside.

wave

To **wave** is to move your hand, usually to say hello or goodbye.

wear

To **wear** something is to put it on your body. These girls are wearing hats, glasses, **jewellery**, and clothes.

wedding

A **wedding** is a special occasion when two people get married.

week

A **week** is a measure of time that is seven days long.

weigh

To **weigh** something is to find out how heavy it is.

wet

When something is **wet**, it is covered with water or another liquid. This dog is wet.

whale

A **whale** is a very large sea animal that breathes air through a hole in the top of its head.

wheat

Wheat is a plant. Its grain is ground up into flour, which is used in other foods.

wheel

A **wheel** is a round object that turns on a rod. Many vehicles move on wheels.

wheelbarrow

A **wheelbarrow** is a small cart with one wheel at the front and two handles. It is used to move things.

wheelchair

A **wheelchair** is a special chair with wheels that helps you to move around if you can't walk.

whisker

Whiskers are the long hairs that grow on the face of some animals.

whisper

To **whisper** is to talk very quietly so that only one person can hear you.

whistle

A **whistle** is a short, hollow piece of metal that makes a loud, high sound when you blow it.

white

White is a colour. Snow and salt are white.

wide

When something is **wide**, it measures a lot from one side to the other.

wind

Wind is air that is moving quickly.

windmill

sail

A **windmill** is a machine with sails that turn in the wind and create power. Windmills were used to grind grain into flour.

window

A **window** is an opening in a **wall** that is filled with glass. Windows let in light and air.

wing

wing

Wings help birds, insects, and aeroplanes to fly.

wire

Wire is thin, metal thread that is often covered with plastic.

witch

A **witch** is an imaginary woman with magical powers.

wizard

A **wizard** is an imaginary man with magical powers.

wolf

A **wolf** is a wild animal that looks like a large dog.

woman

A **woman** is a grown-up girl.

wood

Wood is the hard part of a tree that is used to make tables, chairs, and other things.

wool

Wool is the soft, curly hair of a sheep. Wool is spun into yarn and used for knitting things or making **cloth.**

world

The **world** is the Earth and everything on it.

worm

A **worm** is a long animal with no legs that lives in the ground.

wrinkle

A **wrinkle** is a crease. This dog has wrinkles in its skin.

wrist

Your **wrist** is the joint between your hand and your arm.

write

To **write** is to put words on paper so that people can read them.

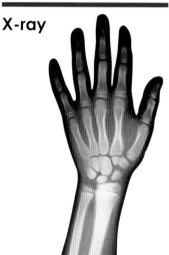

X x

X-ray

An **X-ray** is a special photograph of the inside of your body. Doctors look at X-rays to find out if you are injured or have an illness.

xylophone

A **xylophone** is a musical instrument that has a row of wooden or metal bars. You hit the bars with beaters to make musical sounds.

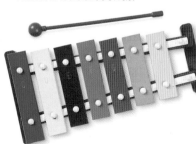

Y y

yellow

Yellow is a colour. Lemons and bananas are yellow.

yacht

A **yacht** is a big, fast boat with sails or an engine.

yawn

To **yawn** is to open your mouth wide and breathe in deeply. You yawn when you are tired or bored.

year

A **year** is a measure of time that lasts 12 months, or 52 weeks, or 365 days.

yoghurt

Yoghurt is a thick, creamy food made from milk. Yoghurt often has fruit mixed with it.

yolk

A **yolk** is the yellow part of an egg.

young

A **young** person is someone who has lived for a short time. This baby is young.

Z z

zebra

A **zebra** is an animal that looks like a horse with black and white stripes on its body.

zero

Zero is the number that comes before one. Zero means none.

zip

A **zip** is used to fasten clothes.

zoo

A **zoo** is a place where animals are kept for people to see. You learn about animals at a zoo.

Dictionary games

See if you can solve all these word puzzles, using your dictionary to help you. At the same time, you can practise looking up words and spellings. You will find all the answers to the puzzles somewhere in the dictionary. The pictures will help you to find the word you are looking for more easily.

Every puzzle has a special box where the first question is answered for you, so you can see what to do. Remember to write your answers down on a piece of paper, not in this book! You can play most of the games on your own, but sometimes you will need a friend to help you. Have fun!

Animal alphabet

These animals should be in alphabetical order, but they have become all mixed up. Use the alphabet at the top of this page to put them back in order.

armadillo

tiger

rabbit

vulture

pelican

elephant

dinosaur

Spelling puzzle

You probably know the names of the things pictured below, but can you spell them? Have a go first, then use your dictionary to see how many you got right.

acrobat

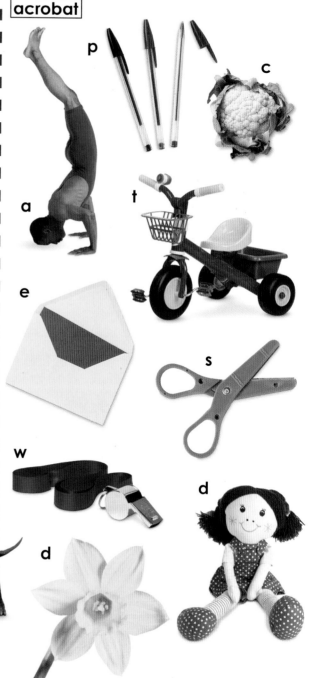

p

c

a

t

e

s

w

d

d

Word detective

Find the right word to answer these questions. You can use the clues to help you, just like a detective does.

> • What do you call a person who breaks into a building to steal something?
> The word begins with the letter **b.**
>
> ## burglar

• What is the name for precious things like gold, silver, coins, and jewels?
Look for the things that sparkle on page 82.

• What can you wear over your face to disguise yourself?
Find the hidden face under **m.**

• What do you call a person who protects people and makes sure laws are obeyed?
Look for a word beginning with **p.**

• What do you wear on your feet to protect them?
Try page 71.

Dictionary lucky dip

This is a game that you can play on your own or with a friend.

1) Think of a letter of the alphabet.

2) Now close your dictionary and try to open it again at exactly the right place to find the letter you have chosen.

You score two points if you find the correct page, and one point if you are close.

Test your memory

▌ Look carefully at all the objects below for one minute. Next close the dictionary and see how many of the things you can remember. Write them down, and then try arranging the words in alphabetical order to make your own little dictionary.

Which one doesn't belong?

If you look carefully at the things below, you will see that in each group there is one thing which doesn't belong. Can you work out which one it is by reading the dictionary definitions?

snake   **beetle**   **bee**

The **snake** is the one that doesn't belong because it is not an insect.

crown   **glove**   **hat**

grapes   **pear**   **carrots**

trumpet   **recorder**   **violin**

Find that word

The answers to the questions below are somewhere in this book. Use the index on page 96 to help you find each answer. Look in the index for each bold word, and it will tell you the page number you want.

> • What is a **mobile phone**?
> A mobile phone is a wireless telephone.

• Who do **guide dogs** help?

• What is a **stallion**?

• How do **firefighters** travel to a fire?

• Why do people send out **invitations**?

• Is there another word for a **rainforest**?

• **Mars** is a planet. Can you name any others?

Sound-alikes

Some words sound the same when you say them, but they have different meanings. With a friend, say these words out loud, and then take turns to look up the meanings. Do you know more pairs of words like this?

bat	**bat**
A **bat** is a kind of stick or racket that is used to hit a ball.	A **bat** is a small, furry animal with wings.

flour	**flower**
nut	**nut**
orange	**orange**
pair	**pear**
right	**write**
scale	**scale**
tie	**tie**

Animal jumble

Here are lots of animals that are all jumbled up.
Answer the questions to find out which animals
make pairs or sets. Remember that the dictionary
definitions will help you.

Which of these birds cannot fly?

toucan

jaguar

sheep

dolphin

goose

cat

crab

lamb

dog

Can you find four baby animals?

How many of these birds can swim?

gosling

penguin

ostrich

Which of these animals live in, or around, water?

starfish

kitten

There are three cats on this page. Can you point to them?

puppy

crocodile

Index of additional words

Acknowledgements

Dorling Kindersley would like to thank the following people for their assistance in the production of this book:

Malavika Talukder, Suneha Dutta, Roma Malik, Neha Chaudhary, Pankaj Deo, Rashmi Rajan, Pragati Nagpal, Archana Ramachandran, Suparna Sengupta, Antara Moitra, Jubbi Francis, Mona Joshi, Neha Gupta, Dharini Ganesh, Parameshwari Sircar, Samira Sood.

Picture Credits

The publisher would like to thank the following for their kind permission to reproduce their photographs:
(Key: a-above; b-below/bottom; c-centre; f-far; l-left; r-right; t-top)

4 Corbis: Boris Roessler / epa (cra). **Fotolia:** Eric Isselée (cr). **Getty Images:** momentimages (bc). **5 Getty Images:** David Madison / Photodisc (cl). **6 Fotolia:** Arto (br). **7 Corbis:** Tetra Images (cr). **Fotolia:** rgbspace (bl). **Getty Images:** Amy Eckert / Photodisc (cra); Ryan McVay / Photodisc (cr). **8 Dorling Kindersley:** Duracell Ltd (cl). **Fotolia:** Nataliya Kashina (bc). **Getty Images:** Jetta Productions / Iconica (c). **9 Fotolia:** iNNOCENt (bl). **Getty Images:** Fuse (cl). **10 Alamy Images:** Baby I Got It (tc). **11 Getty Images:** Johner / Johner Images (br). **12 Getty Images:** Hisham Ibrahim / Photographer's Choice RF (tc). **13 Getty Images:** Glow Images (bl). **14 Corbis:** John Lund / Marc Romanelli / Blend Images (bc). **Dorling Kindersley:** Paul Wilkinson (cla). **Fotolia:** Claude Beaubien (tc). **Getty Images:** Photolove / Cultura (c). **15 Dorling Kindersley:** Stephen Oliver. **16 Corbis:** W. Wisniewski (br). **Getty Images:** Floresco Productions / OJO Images (tl); ImagesBazaar / the Agency Collection (cla); Monica Vinella / Photonica (cra). **17 Getty Images:** Colorblind / Photodisc. **18 Fotolia:** Patrick Hermans (ca). **19 Fotolia:** design56 (bc). **Getty Images:** Michael Blann / Photodisc (clb); Yoshikazu Tsuno / AFP (cka). **20 Dreamstime.com:** Constantin Bogdan Carstina (bl). **Getty Images:** Dimitri Vervitsiotis / Digital Vision (cra). **21 Getty Images:** Peter Dazeley / Photographer's Choice (c); PM Images / Iconica (tl). **22 Dorling Kindersley:** Jamie Marshall (cl). **Fotolia:** Vladimir Mucibabic (bl). **23 Corbis:** Matthias Kulka (tl). **Fotolia:** dinahr (tr). **Getty Images:** Fuse (tl); Roy Ooms / All Canada Photos (cla). **27 Corbis:** Raygun / cultura (cr). **28 Corbis:** Randy Faris (bc). **29 Dorling Kindersley:** Richard Leeney (c). **Getty Images:** Ghislain & Marie David de Lossy / Taxi (ca). **31 Getty Images:** Ove Eriksson / Nordic Photos (clb); Masanobu Hirose / Sebun Photo / amana images (c). **32 Corbis:** Bruce Connolly (bl). **33 Dorling Kindersley:** Lindsey Stock Collection (tc); Comstock Images / Alamy (cr); David Cook / blueshiftstudios / Alamy (br). **Getty Images:** Andrew Olney / Stone (bc). **34 Getty Images:** Steve Debenport / the Agency Collection (tr). **35 Getty Images:** Noel Hendrickson / Digital Vision. **36 Getty Images:** Andrew Geiger / Riser (br). **37 Getty Images:** Studio Box / Photographer's Choice (br). **39 Corbis:** Natalie Tepper / Arcaid (tl). **Getty Images:** Vincenzo Lombardo / Robert Harding World Imagery (cla); Dieter Spannknebel / Photodisc (bc). **40 Dorling Kindersley:** Geoff Brightling / Peter Minister - modelmaker (bc). **41 Corbis:** Andreas Kunert (bl); Ashely Jouhar (tl). **42 Getty Images:** Christoph Martin / Lifesize (tl); Dahl, Per / Johner Images (bc). **43 Getty Images:** David Samuel Robbins / Photographer's Choice (cra). **43 Corbis:** Destinations (cr). **Getty Images:** Robert Glusic / Digital Vision (tc); Michael Hitoshi / Digital Vision (bl). **44 Corbis:** Tim Pannell (br). **Dorling Kindersley:** Philip Dowell (tc); Richard Leeney (cra). **45 Fotolia:** samott (cr). **Getty Images:** Peter Arnold / Digital Vision (bl). **46 Getty Images:** Blend Images / PunchStock (bl). **Getty Images:** Ryan McVay / Photodisc (ca). **47 Dorling Kindersley:** Tim Draper (c). **Dreamstime.com:** Arvind Balaraman (bc). **Fotolia:** Sandra Gligorijevic (crb). **Getty Images:** Lucas Lenci Photo / The Image Bank (cra). **48 Getty Images:** Christopher Bissell / Stone (tc). **50 Corbis:** Dean Conger (br). **Getty Images:** Buena Vista Images / Photodisc (tc). **51 Fotolia:** Alex White (cb). **Getty**

Images: Jack Hollingsworth / Photodisc (bl). **52 Corbis:** Tom & Dee Ann McCarthy (ca). **Getty Images:** Joos Mind / Stone (tl). **53 Corbis:** Robbie Jack (br); TWPhoto (tr). **Fotolia:** leschnyhan (ca). **54 Corbis:** John O'Boyle / Star Ledger (c). **Getty Images:** George Doyle / Stockbyte (cla); Godong / Robert Harding World Imagery (bc). **55 Corbis:** Ludovic Maisant / Hemis (crb). **Dorling Kindersley:** SCPhotos / Dallas and John Heaton / Alamy (br). **Getty Images:** CSA Plastock / CSA Images (cla). **56 Corbis:** Charles Gullung (cr). **Dreamstime.com:** Alekosa (clb). **Getty Images:** Noel Hendrickson / Digital Vision (tr); B2M Productions / Digital Vision (tc). **57 Corbis:** Steve Hix / Somos Images (tl). **Dorling Kindersley:** Judith Miller / Sylvie Spectrum (cb); Stephen Oliver (bc). **Fotolia:** Shawn Hempel (bl). **Getty Images:** Image Source (c). **58 Getty Images:** Lenora Gim / Photonica (ca). **59 Corbis:** Ed Boettcher (cl). **60 Getty Images:** Mark Mann / Taxi (cra). **61 Getty Images:** Billy Hustace / Stone. **62 Getty Images:** Per Breiehagen / The Image Bank (bl). **Getty Images:** Andersen Ross / Digital Vision (clb); Hill Creek Pictures / UpperCut Images. **63 Corbis:** Anderson Ross / Blend Images (cra). **Getty Images:** Dennis Welsh / UpperCut Images. **64 Corbis:** Jose Fuste Raga (c); Warren Jacobi (cr). **Dreamstime.com:** Tamara Bauer (clb). **Getty Images:** Westend61 (tr). **65 Getty Images:** Juan Silva / FoodPix (cra). **66 Corbis:** Pascal Le Segretain / Sygma (crb). **Dorling Kindersley:** Gary Ombler (bl, tr). **Getty Images:** Cameron Davidson / Workbook Stock (c). **67 Corbis:** George Hammerstein (crb). **Getty Images:** Sophia Vourdoukis / Taxi (cla). **68 Corbis:** Denis Scott (cr). **Getty Images:** Alex Cao / Photodisc (cla); Thinkstock Images / Comstock Images (bl). **69 Corbis:** Lew Robertson (clb). **Dorling Kindersley:** Jerry Young (bc). **Getty Images:** Kazuo Honzawa / Sebun Photo / amanaimages; Randy Faris (c); Ed Bock (cr). **Getty Images:** Todd Pearson / Photographer's Choice (tc). **71 Corbis:** JLP / Jose Pelaez (bc). **Getty Images:** Jose Luis Pelaez Inc / Blend Images (cla). **72 Corbis:** Bettmann (bc); Norbert Schaefer (bl). **Getty Images:** Sam Edwards / OJO Images (tr). **73 Getty Images:** Dan Kenyon / Stone (clb). **74 Getty Images:** Jupiterimages / Alamy (cr); Bob Gathany (br); Stephen Oliver (tr). **Getty Images:** Robert Llewellyn / Workbook Stock (crb); Ryan McVay / Photodisc (cb). **76 Dorling Kindersley:** Judith Miller / Freeman's (tl). **Fotolia:** Lucky Dragon USA (br). **NASA:** (cla). **77 Corbis:** Don Hammond / Design Pics (clb). **Dorling Kindersley:** Grain Belt Pictures (cra). **Getty Images:** Taylor S. Kennedy / National Geographic (tr). **78 Corbis:** Larry Williams (cr). **Dorling Kindersley:** Paul Wilkinson (br); Judith Miller / Lyon and Turnbull Ltd. (tl). **Fotolia:** AVAVA (tc); Mykola Velychko (bl); Denis Scott (cb). **Getty Images:** Hisham Ibrahim / Photographer's Choice RF (cra). **79 Corbis:** Owaki - Kulla (cb). **Dorling Kindersley:** Stephen Oliver (ca). **Getty Images:** Yasuhide Fumoto / Digital Vision (cla). **80 Dreamstime.com:** Eslivanova (bc). **81 Getty Images:** PhotoAlto / Sandro Di Carlo Darsa (bc); Chris Stein / Digital Vision (tl). **82 Fotolia:** Brandi Engel (clb). **Getty Images:** Simon Bruty / Photodisc (tr). **83 Dreamstime.com:** Glenda Powers (cl). **Getty Images:** Travelpix Ltd / Stone (tl). **84 Dorling Kindersley:** Stephen Oliver (bc). **Fotolia:** Sergey Mostovoy (tl). **86 Corbis:** Jim Sugar (c). **88 Corbis:** Benelux (cr). **Dorling Kindersley:** Emma Firth (bc); Stockbyte / Photolibrary (cr). **90 Corbis:** Yoav Levy / MedNet (cr). **Fotolia:** GRod (ca). **Getty Images:** Tony Arruza / Stone (br)

Jacket Credits

Front: Alamy: Melba Photo Agency

All other images © Dorling Kindersley
For further information see: www.dkimages.com